Summary

of

Breath
The New Science of a
Lost Art

By James Nestor

Genius Reads

Note to readers:

This is an unofficial summary of James Nestor's {"Breath: The New Science of a Lost Art"} designed to enrich your reading experience.

Legal & Disclaimer

The information contained in this book and its contents is not designed to replace or take the place of any form of medical or professional advice; and is not meant to replace the need for independent medical, financial, legal, or other professional advice or services, as may be required. The content and information in this book has been provided for educational and entertainment purposes only.

The content and information contained in this book has been compiled from sources deemed reliable, and it is accurate to the best of the Author's knowledge, information, and belief. However, the Author cannot guarantee its accuracy and validity and cannot be held liable for any errors and/or omissions. Further, changes are periodically made to this book as and when needed. Where appropriate and/or necessary, you must consult a professional (including but not limited to your doctor, attorney, financial advisor or such other professional advisor) before using any of the suggested remedies, techniques, or information in this book.

Upon using the contents and information contained in this book, you agree to hold harmless the Author from and against any damages, costs, and expenses, including any legal fees potentially resulting from the application of any of the information provided by this book. This disclaimer applies to any loss, damages or injury caused by the use and application, whether directly or indirectly, of any advice or information presented, whether for breach of contract, tort, negligence, personal injury, criminal intent, or under any other cause of action.

You agree to accept all risks of using the information presented inside this book.

You agree that by continuing to read this book, where appropriate and/or necessary, you shall consult a professional (including but not limited to your doctor, attorney, or financial advisor or such other advisor as needed) before using any of the suggested remedies, techniques, or information in this book.

Download Your Free Gift

Before you go any further, why not pick up a free gift from me to you?

Smarter Brain – a 10-part video training series to help you develop higher IQ, memory, and creativity – FAST!

www.Geniusreads.com

Table of Contents

Introduction

SUMMARY OF BREATH BY JAMES NESTOR. Breath by James Nestor is first an exploratory guidebook that describes and teaches us the lost art and science of breathing. It is also a history book that educates us on our ancestors' breathing practices and lifestyle that ensured they remained mostly healthy and more resilient than the current generation. The book tells us how our ability to breathe has deteriorated over the ages, and why our cavemen ancestors didn't snore. James Nestor wants us to understand that breathing goes beyond the simple act of inhaling and exhaling. This book explores the transformation that occurs inside our bodies when we breathe.

For most people, breathing is an automated process required to keep them alive. For James Nestor, breathing, if well understood, is a way to develop the body, build the mind, and grow stronger. Beyond just breathing, how we also breathe matters. Having suffered some respiratory problems, James Nestor admits that joining a breathing class and learning some breathing techniques gave him remarkable relief and, in some cases, cure even over drug, inhaler, a mix of supplements, or diet.

However, James Nestor notes that breathing, like any therapy or medication, can't do everything. It's not going to replace medicine or drugs. Breathing techniques are best suited to serve as preventative maintenance, a way to retain balance in the body so that milder problems don't blossom into more severe health issues. They can also serve as corrective measures to correct some respiratory-related anomalies.

Most of the book's assertions are backed by medical and scientific proof and research, which James Nestor references throughout the book.

Breath is divided into three parts and ten chapters. Part one discloses why some breathing styles might be harmful. James Nestor explains this by sharing his experiences while partaking in an experiment to determine the effect of some breathing style in the body. In part two, James Nestor teaches us how to breathe better. Part three explains some breathing techniques and how these can be best practiced.

Part I

The Worst Breathers In The Animal Kingdom

SUMMARY OF BREATH BY JAMES NESTOR. In Chapter One of Breath, James Nestor describes his experience while partaking in a breathing experiment. The experiment initiated by Dr. Jayakar Navak, a nasal and sinus surgeon, was to determine if anything changed in people's brains and bodies if they changed their breathing style.

Growing up, James Nestor had respiratory challenges, which he suffered up until adulthood. He attributes this majorly to his feeding habit from when he was a baby. According to him, being bottle-fed at six months and weaned onto jarred commercial foods meant that he wasn't chewing as much as possible. The lack of chewing associated with this soft diet stunted bone development in his dental arches and sinus cavity, leading to chronic nasal congestion. At age 15, he was fed on even smoother, highly processed foods consisting mostly of white bread, sweetened fruit juices, canned vegetables, Steak-Umms, Velveeta sandwiches, microwave taquitos, Hostess Sno Balls, and Reggie! Bars. This only worsened the problem as his mouth became underdeveloped and could not contain 32 permanent teeth. Some of his teeth had to be removed because they grew crooked, and years of orthodontics meant that his mouth grew smaller. By the time he was between his 20s to 30s, his breathing had become worse and dysfunctional. According to James Nestor, these experiences had prompted him into an active search for a solution so he could at least breathe better.

Dr. Navak, as James Nestor reveals, is the chief of rhinology research at Stanford and was focused on understanding the hidden power of the nose. And just like James Nestor, Navak believes that the nose is much more than an ancillary organ. As James Nestor notes, Western medicine has a limiting and sometimes wrong understanding of the function of the nose. This incorrect understanding stems from the belief that if people can't breathe out of their nose, then the mouth should handle that function.

Navak discovered that those dunes, stalactites, and marshes inside the human head orchestrate many vital functions for the body. He believes the nose is so important that the body would not function normally without using the nose. This had prompted an experiment in which James Nestor was a volunteer. Navak was on a mission to find out how the body would function without using the nose.

James Nestor revealed that he had his nostrils blocked for the experiment and spent the next ten days breathing through his mouth. He further reveals that Forty percent of today's population suffers from chronic nasal obstruction, and around half of these numbers are habitual mouth breathers, with females and children suffering the most. The causes include dry air to stress, inflammation of allergies, and pollution to pharmaceuticals. As he noted, much of the blame can be placed on the ever-shrinking real estate in front of the human skull.

Mouth Breathing

SUMMARY OF BREATH BY JAMES NESTOR. Breathing through the mouth is a new health disaster. Nasal breathing warms, humidifies, and cleans the incoming air. Up to 95 to 99% of bacteria, viruses, dust, and other air pollutants get trapped on the nasal airways' moist surfaces. They are designed to be narrow and long. During mouth breathing, the irritants and pollutants can travel to bronchi, lungs, and blood.

Self-test. If you sometimes keep your mouth open at rest, measure your CP after keeping your mouth open for about 20 minutes. Compare this number with your CP when your mouth is closed after another 20 minutes.

Poor Posture

Poor posture (the norm for modern people) also results in reduced CPs.

Practically, slouching means that the CP is below, at least, 25 to 30 seconds.

Self-test. Measure your CP when you are relaxed with good posture. Spend 15 to 20 minutes in an awkward or uncomfortable (e.g., slouching) position with chronically tense muscles. Measure your new CP.

Infections, stress, and intense emotions, feeling under pressure, having physiological stress (e.g., bacterial or viral infections), and when experiencing many strong emotions cause a drop in CPs.

Abnormal Thermoregulation

Having extra clothes and being in a too-warm environment for a long time are other factors that interfere with oxygen supply. After 10 to 20 minutes in such conditions, the CP can decrease by 5 to 10 or more seconds.

Self-test. Measure your CP in normal conditions. Spend 15 to 20 minutes in warm or hot conditions. You can do that by wearing more clothes. Check changes in your CP.

All these practical observations produce many questions. Why does overeating reduce oxygenation? Why is sleeping too long, or on the back, or with open mouth dangerous? How does stress hamper oxygenation? These and many other questions have a solid scientific explanation. All these effects influence one central factor that directly regulates Oxygen transport to tissues: the way we breathe.

One can observe that the modern man often has his/her mouth open (while sitting, standing, reading, working, walking, exercising, etc.). Breathing through one's mouth reduces Carbon Dioxide (CO_2)

levels in the lungs and, hence, the whole body. Why? Nasal breathing creates more resistance to airflow. Hence, we can tolerate higher CO_2 concentrations in the lungs and blood since more work to ventilate the lungs is required to keep the same CO_2 levels during nasal breathing. The difference is especially large during physical exercise. In addition, mouth breathing makes the volume of the dead space smaller. (The dead space is the air reservoir between the lungs and outer air.) This intermediate reservoir helps us to have higher CO_2 concentrations in the lungs.

Finally, nasal passages produce Nitric Oxide (NO), a gas that is to be inhaled into the lungs and absorbed in the blood for dilation of blood vessels. Many heart patients use nitroglycerine and some other heart drugs, which release nitric oxide into the bloodstream. However, heart patients often breathe through the mouth; thereby, losing their own best source for NO produced naturally by the body.

Similarly, when the nose becomes blocked, people open their mouths for breathing. This makes their problem worse. The nose can get completely blocked due to constriction of small blood vessels and reduced blood supply.

Was the situation in relation to mouth breathing differently in the past? To detect historical changes, you can investigate photos and movies made, for example, 30 or more years ago. Was it reasonable, then, for people to have open mouths for breathing?

Is physical inactivity a factor?

Our primitive ancestors were physically active for 6 to 12 hours every day.

We, on average, are active for about 1 to 2 hours per day or often less. Too little physical exercise depresses metabolism and oxygen transport, gradually causing chronic hyperventilation. Russian practical observations revealed that, if a healthy individual (with about 60 s CP) has only 1 to 2 hours or less of daily physical activity, his/her breathing will be getting worse and worse. The CP can drop down to about 30 to 35 s or even less.

Note that even during physical exercise, we should keep our mouths closed. Unfortunately, it is rare to meet a person who exercises with his/her mouth shut all the time.

How healthy should we be to exercise? Practical experience of Soviet and Russian doctors revealed that exercise is inadvisable for low CPs (below about 20 s). Physical activity does not provide maximum benefits when people breathe through their mouths while exercising. In these cases, CO_2 stores usually get smaller. Breathing and the CP can get worse for many hours after such an exercise.

When the CP is critically low (as with severely sick people), practice becomes dangerous.

Part II

Nose

SUMMARY OF BREATH BY JAMES NESTOR. This step is essential to breathe correctly. Unless you're doing a vigorous, herculean exercise, try breathing through your nostrils. This helps filter out pollutants, allergens, and toxins when we inhale, and it heats and humidifies the air. When we breathe through the mouth, the volume of air increases markedly, leading to that habit of excessive breathing and increased anxiety.

As a colophon: it also dries the mouth, and we can acquire dental problems. Needless to say, more.

If you start breathing well, this will help you:

Stop snoring. Surely, it is your partner's dream, who asks every time he has to blow out the candles for his birthday. Snoring can be associated with excessive inhalation due to increased air volume and vibrations. It can lead to non-restful sleep, fatigue, a dry mouth, sore throat, or headache. Solution? Sleep on your side and avoid eating a lot of drinking alcohol just before bed.

Eliminate stress. We have already seen that breathing is closely related to nervousness. Restful sleep and being lively and calm will help you breathe well, but when do you notice stress knocking on your door? Take some time to distract yourself, go for a walk. Synchronize the rhythm of your steps with that of your breathing, not to do it irregularly. Having anxiety makes us breathe fast, but breathing incorrectly increases our chances of suffering anxiety, so stop for a moment, think about your diaphragm, calm down, and, now, breathe.

Exhale

SUMMARY OF BREATH BY JAMES NESTOR. We must breathe through the nose, as long as there are no difficulties that prevent it, such as problems with the nostrils, mucus, being a smoker ..., since we have natural filters that prevent the entry of dust and hostile organisms such as bacteria and viruses. It also regulates the temperature and humidity of the air that enters our lungs. When inhaling, air enters the lungs, reaching the blood oxygen and traveling to the cells. These consume Oxygen during the process of making energy for our body and dispose of Carbon Dioxide, which will do the same way but in reverse. It passes into the blood from the cells, reaches the lungs, and returns to the air through respiration. We do this process without thinking and unconsciously almost always.

Paying attention during the day to how we breathe and how it affects our body gives us multiple physical and energy benefits. It is the so-called conscious breathing, and it not only helps us to make the energy flow balanced through our body, but it also relaxes, reduces anxiety, increases vitality, improves mood and even if we do it during meals, it helps with proper digestion and better assimilation of nutrients.

An excellent exercise to become aware of breathing is as follows:

· Breathe in deeply and slowly through your nose

· Keep the air in the lungs for a few seconds

· Exhale through the nose releasing the air as slowly as possible

· Keep the lungs airless for a few seconds

· Start the cycle again and repeat the actions several times

Breathing also has therapeutic uses through various types of exercises based on the same points explained but varying the residence time in each of the phases of the cycle (seconds clear). These exercises serve to calm, purify, tone, balance, maintain and increase lung capacity, help in respiratory diseases, maintain the muscles in general, and slow disease progression.

An essential factor to consider when breathing consciously is the ionization of the air. Ionization is a natural, physical, or chemical process by which ions are produced. Ions are molecules or atoms that contain an electric charge called an electron. Depending on the number of electrons gained or lost, ions are positive or negative. However, now is not the time to do a physics class, so I'll get to the point.

The ionization that brings benefits to the human body is harmful and is the one that helps us breathe better and more deeply. In contrast, positive ionization can be detrimental to humans.

In nature, ionization processes are constant, for example, positive ions are formed when different atmospheric fronts rub, and the first ones to detect it are animals. However, some susceptible people notice the formation of negative ions through discomfort and bone pain, scarring, or headache. It should also be borne in mind that pollution positively ionizes the air so that in large cities and industrial areas, the air and being of lower quality, will be undoubtedly ionized and can cause health problems. Another factor to consider is the incorporation of chemistry in the food industry that introduces positive ions into the body and, as a direct consequence, has the appearance of free radicals.

Negative ionization in the air is generated for different reasons:

· Storms and other meteorological phenomena such as lightning and wind

· Right after it rains as the rainwater carries the electrons out of the storm

· Natural radiation or radioactivity from land in forests and mountains

· Where sea waves break like rocks and groins

· Rivers very full of water and waterfalls

All these natural causes generate negative ionization. We must go outside the house and breathe consciously to take advantage of benefits such as improved mood and increased physical and mental vitality. We must also be aware of what positive ionization in the air hurts us, but always keeping in mind that everyone lives where they live, and if you live in the city, you should not worry about it. But that depends if we are aware and leave when we can breathe outside the contaminated areas. The walks and excursions to the mountain or the beach will help us to maintain health.

Slow

SUMMARY OF BREATH BY JAMES NESTOR. If we observe our breathing, we will realize that the air we inhale only expands the upper part of the lungs in many cases. If we look at a baby, we will see that the air he inhales swells his tummy. Over time, we tend to lose that kind of calm, deep breathing. Regaining abdominal breathing is the goal of this technique.

By making the air reach the abdomen, noticing how it swells, we are using all the lung capacity; we bring air to the lowest part of the lungs.

It is very important to do it slowly. Counting to five when inhaling, and again five when exhaling, is an adequate rhythm. It is the most straightforward technique to start making you aware of your breathing and is indicated to reduce anxiety.

Retention Techniques

In this practice, you must take a deep inhalation, retain the air in the lungs for the time that passes while we count to ten, and then release the air very slowly. This technique is widely used to discharge tension.

Reverse retention breathing consists of doing ten slow breathing exercises, expelling on the eleventh exhalation all the air that we are capable of. The lungs are then kept empty for as long as possible, to inhale normally again. This exercise is completed 10 to 15 times. It is indicated for insomnia problems.

The technique of increased respiratory rate

This technique has variants, but basically, it consists of achieving a respiratory cycle of 2 seconds, 1 to inhale, and 1 to exhale. It is used briefly and in cases where we feel out of energy, and an increase in vitality is required. It is the respiratory substitute for the stimulating effect of coffee, for example.

The most fun variant is doing this type of breathing while mentally visualizing that laziness and apathy are discharged with each exhalation. People should avoid this technique with a tendency to anxiety or high blood pressure problems because it increases the heart rate. It is also recommended to do it at first under supervision.

Less

SUMMARY OF BREATH BY JAMES NESTOR. Did you know that there are specific ways of breathing that could contribute to stress reduction? At first, it may be somewhat complicated to practice the four techniques that we teach you in this chapter. But, over time, you will not only get it, but you will feel less tense.

Surely, you will have experienced a situation of stress or anxiety on more than one occasion. And very probably you have also noticed that, in those situations, you breathe in a fast and uncomfortable way. And, it is not for less.

Stress and anxiety are coping mechanisms. They are intended to help us evade a situation that the brain interprets as harmful or dangerous. It should also be remembered that the sympathetic nervous system's response to these feelings is very intense.

Not for pleasure, in these situations, the heart accelerates, the pulsations increase, and we breathe irregularly. It seems logical then that the risk of suffering heart attacks, angina, and strokes, increases among many other conditions.

But, have you ever wondered why? It should be remembered that bad breath results in our organs, not getting the oxygen they need to function properly. This stress situation for the organism

27

almost always leaves sequels, especially when such situations persist for a long period.

It is imperative to stop to analyze what is happening to us to look for possible solutions. The need to better manage emotions will then prevail. Breathing correctly could be another very useful resource for reducing stress. So, here are four techniques that could help you reach the goal of learning to breathe better.

1. The Square Breath

Square breathing is the simplest of all breathing techniques. It is also known as samavriti pranayama. You could do it in bed, 20 minutes before sleeping. It will help you relax and rest deeply.

Steps:

· Sit on the bed with your back straight and your legs crossed.

· Breathe deeply for 3 minutes, trying to relax.

· Now, breathe in for 3 seconds, hold the air for another 3 seconds. And finally, breathe out for another 3 seconds.

· After a short rest, repeat the same steps, increasing the duration of such intervals to 4 seconds.

As you make this breathing exercises routine a habit, you can increase the time between each step until you reach 7 seconds or 8 seconds.

2. Abdominal Breathing

With square breathing, what you do is inflate your chest. The goal of abdominal breathing is now to focus on breathing on the diaphragm. This is a very effective technique to treat stress, contained tension, and anxiety.

Steps:

· Lie down on the bed or a quilt comfortably.

· Place one hand on your chest and one on your belly.

· Take a deep breath in through your nose for about 3 seconds. You will notice how your belly swells while the upper chest is stretched.

· Then exhale little by little for about 4 seconds.

Ideally, this routine should be performed ten times. Try to do them very slowly. Imagine how the diaphragm will help you focus on this breathing exercise.

3. Alternate Nasal Breathing

Alternative nasal breathing may seem strange to us if we have never practiced it. Therefore, the idea is to practice a little every day. You will gradually notice its benefits. When you get used to it, you will notice not only that it will help you channel and release stress. Also, to direct your attention only to what you are doing.

Steps:

· Sit so that you feel comfortable. However, make sure that your back is straight.

· Relax for a few minutes.

· Bring your right thumb up to your nose to cover the right nostril.

· Take a deep breath through the left nostril.

· When you feel your lungs have filled to the point where you cannot breathe more air, close the left nostril with your right ring finger.

· Exhale through the right nostril.

· Do the same thing again, but in reverse. Once you have taken as much air as possible with the right nostril, close it and exhale through the left nose.

It may seem a little complicated at first. In all likelihood, you will need to be aware of covering one pit and opening the other. However, as you repeat it, the exercise will become more rhythmic and relaxing.

4. Consistent Breathing

Consistent breathing also requires practice and patience. We invite you to always to try it, adapting it to your abilities and personal characteristics. When you have managed to control it, you will feel more comfortable with yourself, and your whole body will thank you.

Consistent breathing consists of breathing five times per minute. In this way, the heart rate is optimized, and you will be able to relax the nervous system. It is an effective way to channel accumulated tension in situations of stress and anxiety. Practicing it will be of great help.

Steps:

· Sit with your back straight.

· Put a clock in front of you.

· The goal is to inspire and expire five times for a single minute. However, it is recommended that you first test your ability to control breathing. If you found that you couldn't distribute them over 1 minute, start by doing 6 or 7 inspirations and expirations.

· However, when you manage to distribute them in just 1 minute, you will feel much better.

Chew

SUMMARY OF BREATH BY JAMES NESTOR. There is also the case of the mouth. For those who have less airway obstruction, the uvula hangs high and visible from top to bottom. However, the deeper the uvula appears in the throat, the higher the risk of airway obstruction. If the tongue overlaps with the molars, it'll also impact breathing.

If you have a more massive neck, you may have airway obstruction during sleep or disorders like sleep apnea. Blockage doesn't start with your throat, uvula, or tongue, but with your mouth. The main thing causing airway obstruction is a mouth that is too small for the face.

For most people, the best way to combat this problem is preventative measures. The first preventative measure of this kind was called the "monobloc," a contraption that moved the jaw back so that the throat could open up and more air could get inside. From there, people began to expand the idea of orthodontic devices by adding components that would straighten the teeth. By expanding the mouth, it allowed teeth to grow in straight.

At some point in the 1940s, it became commonplace to begin removing teeth from the head to create more room in the mouth instead of trying to create more place in the mouth for teeth to grow. Removing teeth only made the mouth smaller, offering less room for people to breathe. Using twin studies, Dr. John Mew found that those who had teeth removed ended up with smaller mouths and more difficulty breathing than those who had mouths expanded.

In recent years, people have begun to take Dr. Mew's findings more seriously, and orthodontists have found that breathing only worsens in most patients who have orthodontic devices. Mew had created the "Biobloc," a modified version of the monobloc. It expanded airways by up to 30% in 6 months.

The first step to expanding airways was to hold the lips together with teeth lightly touching, placing your tongue at the roof of your mouth. Hold your head perpendicular to the body and don't kink the neck. The spine should form a J-shape. Breathe slowly in through the nose and into the abdomen.

Most of us have naturally created an S-shape in our posture due to our tongues getting in the way of our breathing. We've begun to hunch forward slightly to get the breath we need.

One exercise that can help is "mewing". There are videos online you can watch the process. However, the gist is to push the back of the tongue against the back roof of the mouth and move the rest of the tongue forward, like a wave, until the tip hits behind the front teeth. It should look like you are trying not to throw up.

One doctor, Belfor, has concluded that the idea that we lose bones as we age is a "total bullshit". He believes that we can grow bone at any age, as long as we have stem cells. We produce stem cells to build more maxilla bone in the face by engaging the masseter—or by clamping down on the back molars repeatedly. The more we chew, the more bones we grow and the better we'll breathe.

Belfor created his version of the biobloc, but this one left room for a chewing mechanism to help grow bone density in the mouth. This would allow the patient to grow bone density while also expanding the mouth to leave room for better breathing.

When measured, jaws over the course of the last 300 years have decreased in size by almost 20%. This is directly related to the decline of chewing.

Some researchers sought to find if the same phenomenon was true with animals as it was with people. They changed the food of pigs to see if their faces would narrow and teeth would crowd as a result of the food change. What happened was much the same as humans. Pigs began having breathing problems due to the change in their mouth structures.

However, even with all the research, that chewing is what's causing our mouth deformities, the U.S. National Institute of Health still doesn't recognize it as the leading cause of crooked teeth and other deformations of the airway. Instead, their website claims that it's hereditary and that other causes could include thumb-sucking, injury, or a tumor.

After the author tried Belfor's method, he gained 1,658 cubic millimeters of new bone in his cheeks and right eye sockets, as well as 118 cubic millimeters of bone along his nose and 178 along his upper jaw. His jaw changed alignment and was more balanced, and he was able to breathe more clearly and without sinus obstruction.

Our noses and mouths are not predetermined at birth, and we can reverse the clock on much of the damage we do to them. We need to work on gaining proper posture, hard chewing, and mewing to do so. This will clear up the obstruction and we will be able to breathe peacefully.

Part III

More, on Occasion

SUMMARY OF BREATH BY JAMES NESTOR. While the earlier parts of the book have focused on techniques that you could do anywhere, and that anyone could benefit from, the following are more specific to individual bodies. These are more extreme techniques that under some circumstances, could cause a need for medical care, but under most, will cause a radically transformed life. These techniques are called breathing + and build on the foundations already set.

The first technique is for those who have manic breathing, and was originally developed for soldiers during the Civil War. The heart rate was a bit irregular and rapid for these people, a condition now known as Irritable Heart Syndrome. It's a disorder of the sympathetic nervous system.

The parasympathetic nervous system stimulates relaxation and restoration, like the kind you get when you sleep or eat a big meal. It's the "feed and breed" system because it prepares your body to eat and prepares your body for sex. A lot of the lungs are covered with nerves that relate to this system, so the more you breathe in, the more this system is activated.

The second half is the sympathetic nervous system, and it has the opposite role. It stimulates the signals to the organs to get them ready for action. These nerves are at the top of the lungs so they can respond to short, hasty breaths. It's where the negative energy you feel when you get an adrenaline rush comes from, and it causes an increase in your heart rate. It also helps ease pain and keep blood from leaving our bodies when we're injured.

Our bodies are built to go back and forth between the two, but not spend a lot of time in the sympathetic nervous system. However, the first technique involves forcing your body to stay in a prolonged sense of this system using a breathing technique called Inner Fire Meditation. When used correctly, there would be intense surges of energy.

Soldiers experience unconscious stress; however, this first technique involves being conscious of your stress and using it to your advantage. It's especially useful for people like Navy SEALs, martial arts fighters, and those in dangerous professions who can teach themselves how to breathe well during crises. When a crisis occurs, our heart rate slows, as does circulation and organ function.

In order to fix this, you have to stimulate the vagus nerve, the root of the automatic sensory system. Since breathing is an automatic function we can't control, we have to teach ourselves to breathe slowly and open up communication. However, breathing fast and heavy on purpose will flip the vagal response and show us in a stressed state. If we turn on this heavy stress, we will be more relaxed later than the body tries to balance.

Mixing heavy breathing with regular cold exposure releases the stress hormones adrenaline, cortisol, and nor-epinephrine on command, enabling the immune system. Breathing correctly can help many immune-suppression diseases, as well.

To practice this technique, start by finding a quiet place and lying flat on your back. Place a pillow under your head and take the deepest breath you can, letting the air into the pit of your stomach. Let it back out just as quickly, and keep doing this for 30 cycles. Breathe through your nose if you can, or pursed lips. Inhale so that the air fills your belly first, then your chest. Then let it out in the same way.

Then, exhale on the last breath until there's about a quarter of the breath left in your lungs and try to hold it for 15 seconds. Start the heavy breathing again and do this cycle 4 to 5 more times. Then, add in some cold exposure like an ice bath or a cold shower. Alternating like this allows the body to exert the energy needed.

In addition to the Tummo technique described above, there is another heavy breathing technique. This technique is called the Holotropic Breathwork technique and was created by a man named Stainislav Grof. The purpose is to restart the mind.

Grof's technique was a heightened version of the Tummo technique. His technique was to lay in a room with loud music playing and breathe as hard and quickly as you could for three hours. This helped patients access subconscious and unconscious thoughts, unlocking the mind to get back to being calm. However, some patients found that they suffered nervous breakdowns. As a result, psychiatrists often use it to help patients have breakthroughs.

Some patients find that this method only brings about calm feelings and a surrender.

Deep breathing exercises provide good stress and tension release through the symbolic exhaling of "bad energy." However, what is important is how we breathe and not just to stop what you are doing and begin slowly deep breathing. There are techniques to properly bring the air into the lungs to be used correctly in our bodies. Breathing calmly regulates your heart rate. The point of proper breathing is to breathe slowly, to breathe out as long as possible, and to focus on the exhaling and not the inhaling. In overwhelming situations, we tend to breathe fast and shallow or take deep breaths, which are both wrong and can make us lightheaded and dizzy. Abdominal breathing has been proved to be more relaxing than chest breathing. The exercise goes like this: put one palm on your abdomen and the other on your chest, and then try breathing in

40

through your nostrils and breathing out through the mouth that forms a shape, as if blowing a whistle; your hand that the hand on the chest stays static. This improves blood flow in the lungs and leads blood to the heart, relieving the chest pressure. Repeat 6 times a minute, with breathing being prolonged. With slow and prolonged breathing, your brain increases neurotransmitters (GABA), which is responsible for relieving from stress and calmness. Other exercises for proper breathing are breathing 4-7-8, roll breathing, and morning breathing. They could be combined with progressive muscle relaxation.

Progressive muscle relaxation is a method that includes slow contraction and release of each part of the body in complete calmness and silence, with corrected breathing. While breathing in, you should contract specific muscles and relax them as you breathe out. This technique allows you to be more aware of different states when relaxed and contracted and become easier to maintain a relaxed position instead of a stiff, contracted, tense motion. The technique isn't particularly tiresome, but you should avoid some muscles at any sign of hurt or exhaustion. The position in which you should work these exercises can be either in a comfortable chair with arm support or lying on your back. There are stages of intentional relaxation and these are tense and release, lightly tense and release, and only release.

Visualization is a technique that uses creating an image with visual or other features that remind of peace, calmness, and happy times. It may help close your eyes and try to think of many characteristics of the happy place and sounds, smells, feelings, as many details as possible, and some personal things that calm you down. Visualization may be in the form of a short film with a specific plot and characters. The display's subject is very individual and with time, a person will develop skills to include as many details possible, with more and more characteristics and sound included. At first, this technique is mastered in a calm environment. Still, with time, as person becomes has more control over the visualization technique, he/she could master performing it even in any situation. This technique is sometimes referred to as day-dreaming. Subjects may include some future or desired situations or past conflicts that could have been managed differently. The mechanism in which this actually works is by visualizing relaxing and soothing feelings. You may actually trick your brain that it is happy and at peace and create the body-mind state as if it was really happening.

Biofeedback therapy has a different approach than all the others, and it requires a specialist and an institution to perform it. The technique revolves around control over body functions that aren't normally controllable. Biofeedback therapy involves using electrodes to provide information about heart rate, breathing rate and depth, blood pressure, and muscle relaxation/tension. A professional is there to give advice on exercises and operate electrodes connected to a monitor. A person does the exercises to self-induce lower blood pressure, lower heartbeat rate, and to evaluate his/her own breathing properly. Along with these exercises, he/she performs tension of the muscles and relaxation. A person sees how both of them look on the monitor and learns to control both of them. Biofeedback therapy can be used for treatment of pain, headaches, anxiety, and illnesses with organic background.

Massage therapy was from ancient days used along with other techniques to bond body and mind and create an aggregation of the two in calmness and peace. Massage techniques are best performed by physiotherapists and can be beneficial for all of the inner organs. It can help decrease the sympathetic nerve response to stress. Either way, there are many types of massage: sports, orthopedic, and therapeutical. They are used for different purposes: for enhancing the blood flow, and therefore relieving pain, or softening stiff muscles of the back, because of stress and tension. Its effects also revolve around producing certain hormones (serotonin and oxytocin) and the decrease of cortisol - a stress hormone, which all make us feel more relaxed. Many massage experts claim about proper transfer of unwanted energy to a more desirable one. Stress effects should be transferred into healthy energy, which produces a motivated and relaxed individual. The technique is carefully performed and has two effects: through physical and psychological relaxation. The effects appear from stimulation of receptors located in the deep tissue below the skin that send impulses to the brain and create a response. With kneading techniques, proprioceptors in deep tissue are stimulated, and then they induce sending of the impulses farther to the brain. Kneading needs to cover at least 50% of massage time. In this technique, a part of skin is pinched, held, and massaged with the fingers to stimulate the receptors. Other techniques that should be included are gliding (in direction of the blood flow), trigger point massage of the affected tissue with knots in muscles, long strokes, etc. Swedish massage is the most frequently performed Western technique for stress relief, even though there are Eastern-based massages as well.

Hold It

SUMMARY OF BREATH BY JAMES NESTOR. One researcher embarked on a cruel experiment with monkeys. Kling removed the amygdala from monkey's brains and found that all of those monkeys died within a week. The reason was that the amygdala houses fear in the brain, and once the monkeys were no longer afraid, they couldn't tell what a predator was and what prey was. Without fear, survival was impossible.

There was also a young woman born in the United States who had an impaired amygdala. As a result, she could experience every emotion except fear and fear's secondary emotions, such as anxiety. Fear is the basis of all anxiety and so on; a neuronal level, anxiety, and phobias are caused by an overactive amygdala.

Researchers studied this woman to see if they could make her feel fear when faced with physiologically harmful, not just psychologically. They placed a carbon dioxide mask over her mouth, which made her feel like she was drowning. Immediately, she exhibited the first signs of fear that she'd had in decades. Researchers repeated this on other patients with a damaged amygdala and found the same result. This led them to conclude that there must be more than one place in the body that processes the emotion of fear, and this other place must be triggered by physiological danger.

45

The need to breathe is activated from the central chemoreceptors, which are located at the base of the brain stem. Chemoreception has been around since the beginning of life, since early aerobic life had to avoid it to be able to function. It is these reactors that stimulate the suffocation feeling that you felt holding your breath.

Chemoreceptor flexibility is what distinguishes a good athlete from a bad athlete, since athletes can train their chemoreceptors to withstand fluctuations in carbon dioxide without panicking. Our mental health relies on this flexibility, as well. We're conditioned to panic when we can't get a breath or think we won't be able to breathe, but the reason is that it's generated by chemoreceptors and breathing is profound.

18% of Americans suffer from some form of anxiety or panic. This research shows us that instead of treating them with medicine that affects the amygdala, researchers should find medicine that helps with the chemoreceptors.

Breath-holding is associated almost entirely with disease. However, this isn't the case. The breath-holding that occurs in sleep is unconscious—it's something that happens to our bodies, not something that we control. However, there are forms of breath-holding that are conscious, like those done by ancient tribes.

The researcher that found the link between chemoreceptors and carbon dioxide now believes that carbon dioxide can cure anxiety. Rather than working on breathing treatments, these people inhaled some of the gas, flexed their chemoreceptors back to normal, and continued with their day.

Some physicians even bottle up carbon dioxide and put it into an inhaler. It's been used to treat strokes, pneumonia, asthma, and asphyxia in newborn babies, and to help with those who have been exposed to a lot of smoke. Higher blends are used for those with anxiety, epilepsy, and schizophrenia. Then, the medicine world changed and began relying more on pills and creams than inhalers.

Few people still research the effects of an inhalant of carbon dioxide, but the data has never been disproven. Breathing techniques can still be used to treat those who have anxiety. People with anorexia or panic or obsessive-compulsive disorders seem to consistently have low carbon dioxide levels and a greater fear of holding their breath.

Researchers found that panic, like asthma, follows an increase in breathing volume and rate, thereby lowering the body's amount of carbon dioxide. If you can get the carbon dioxide back in the body, you can cut off panic and anxiety through slow and heavy breaths. The best way to solve a panic attack is not to take a deep breath, but to hold the breath you do have. Many people report that they feel discomfort initially, but the calm feeling follows and lasts for days after.

The author decides to try this method out himself. He remembers the conditioning he did with Olsson back in Sweden, where he had to run to the point where his body was fueled by carbon dioxide.

He tries the method, immediately feeling the same panic that others do when inhaling carbon dioxide. His heart rate increases and then decreases on exhale, and his oxygen levels stay consistent. He remarks that he "feels like a fighter pilot on a stealth mission", his adrenaline is so high. However, the sense of calm doesn't change, and he attributes that to his mouth-breathing exercises and how he has raised his resting carbon dioxide levels.

He repeats the process multiple times to train his chemoreceptors and increase their flexibility.

Fast, Slow, and Not at All

SUMMARY OF BREATH BY JAMES NESTOR. The author goes to meet a man named DeRose, who studies and teaches a practice that is an aerobic exercise used in conjunction with breathing and thinking. He wants to know why the different breathing methods seem to affect the physiological reactions of the body.

He wants to find out why Holotrophic Breathwork makes the body have almost hallucinatory effects. Since nobody can explain it, he wants to turn to someone who practices the ancient exercises for help. Since all of his breath work started in ancient texts, he figures DeRose is the right place to start.

One of the yoga world's biggest words is "prana", which means "life force". It's the theory of atoms and how they relate to energy in the body, and was first documented back in India and China about three millennia ago. The Chinese called it ch'i and believed the body had different channels for energy.

Many ancient cultures believed that breathing well was essential to a good life. They are often depicted in breathing poses, with arms outstretched and hands with thumbs in front placed on their knees. Usually, their legs are crossed or the feet' soles are joined with the toes pointing down. This was a common posed used in ancient times to facilitate breathing, and it is often memorialized in art from

49

the time period. These are the first artifact to show "yogic" postures in human history, and they're found in the Indus region.

When the drought hit in 2000 BCE, these people began to migrate and find new places to stay, bringing their form of breathing with them and marrying them with the religious texts they now occupied. The earliest yoga practices have always been a science of sitting still and building prana through breathing, not of moving into various poses.

Modern yoga and ancient yoga, then, are very different. Modern yoga is an evolved form of ancient yoga, and both have similar healing benefits. However, yoga's original practices were never designed to cure medical problems, but rather, to give healthy people a chance to increase their potential.

One other method is that of Sudarshan Kriya, an old practice that has been around since 400 BCE, and was used by many famous leaders at the time, including Krishna and Jesus Christ. It was designed out of the same practices as Tunno, and requires more than 40 minutes of intensive breathing. Doing this, however, builds up too much prana before your body can adapt to it.

Ancient yogis spent a lot of time on these techniques to control their energy and distribute it well within their bodies. It takes many months or years to master it, and modern breathers try to cut corners and end up failing at it. The key is to slowly absorb what it has to offer and give it time to work.

One of the best tips is to concentrate on making your breath one fluid movement, from inhale to exhale. This is the instruction that comes from the Sudarshan Kriya. It feels similar to a wave.

Most techniques are similar, and all showcase the best way for your body to breathe. They're repackaged in different cultures, at different times and for different reasons. Trying any of them gives us a chance to stretch our lungs and improve our physical health both for now and the future.

A Last Gasp

SUMMARY OF BREATH BY JAMES NESTOR. We deal with several stressful situations daily—work, family, education, friendships, romantic relationships, driving on the interstate, just walking down the street. These and more are all situations that can have our minds racing and keep us on our tiptoes. There has been a lot of focus on the negative contribution of stress on the cardiovascular system, obesity, diabetes, high blood pressure, and mental health to name a few, but how often is the effect of stress on breathing shared? Not enough I would assume, but a change in breathing is one of the first indications that a person needs to make a change.

One of the first things that change in your breathing when you are in a stressful situation is how you breathe. When you are breathing healthily, you breathe through your diaphragm, a muscle in the base of the chest that separates the abdomen from the chest. The diaphragm flattens and contracts when a person inhales, which causes a vacuum effect. This pulls air into the lungs. This muscle relaxes to push air out of the lungs when a person exhales.

Stress causes you to breathe through your chest instead of the diaphragm, sending a signal to your brain that you are not relaxed, and you might be in danger. This induces a fight-or-flight response and the production of the stress hormone, cortisol. This causes you to take short and erratic breaths and your muscles tense and constrict in preparation of fight or flight.

Your entire respiratory system, which allows us to breathe and includes organs such as the lungs, diaphragm, and nose, goes haywire and causes your heart rate to quicken and spike blood pressure. This compounds the negative effect on your respiratory system and causes you to breathe even faster and shallower.

This situation can escalate into a condition called hyperventilation, which is a panic response to stress, fear, or phobia. During normal breathing situations, a balance of inhalation and exhalation allows the intake of oxygen and the expulsion of carbon dioxide to occur in the balance as well. This balance is disturbed during hyperventilation because a person breathes very fast, exhaling more than they inhale. This translates into the person eliminating more carbon dioxide from the body than inhaling oxygen into the body. While carbon dioxide is a waste product of the body, it needs to be expelled controlled. Low levels of carbon dioxide cause the blood vessels that supply the brain to constrict. This means that not enough blood will be supplied to the brain, and a person will experience initial symptoms like tingling of the fingers and lightheadedness. Other hyperventilation symptoms include dizziness, shortness of breath, a lump in the throat, nausea, and confusion. If hyperventilation is not controlled and becomes severe, the person may lose consciousness.

Luckily, consciously controlling your breathing can reverse all these negative effects. The first thing you need to do is become aware of your response to stress. Next, you need to encourage breathing through your diaphragm instead of your chest. Here is a quick method to do this:

1. If possible, remove yourself from the situation that is causing you stress.

2. Sit comfortably in a quiet room and close your eyes to block out the rest of the world and concentrate internally. Tell yourself to relax and visualize that state in your mind.

3. Slowly and gently inhale air through your nose to fill your lower lungs. You will know that you have done this correctly if your stomach expands while your upper chest remains still. This is alternately called belly breathing.

4. Hold your breath for the count of three, and then exhale through pursed lips. Breathe out as slowly as possible. Breathing out through pursed lips makes it easier for the lungs to function since it promotes diagrammatic breathing and improves the balance of oxygen intake and carbon dioxide outtake.

Consciously relax the muscles in your face, jaw, shoulders, stomach, and thighs.

5. Repeat steps 3 and 4 about ten more times. Concentrate on your emotions. Allow yourself to feel the negative ones such as anger and sadness, and then breathe them away.

6. Open your eyes again.

If hyperventilation occurs, modify the steps above to breathe into a paper bag or cupped hands and hold your breath for 10 to 15 seconds instead.

As you calm your breath, the following things will happen:

• Your breath will slow.

• Your heart rate will go down, and your blood pressure will decrease.

• Your intake of oxygen and expulsion of carbon dioxide will once again become balanced.

• Cortisol levels in the blood will decrease.

• Muscle tension will decrease.

• Your mind calms.

Also, you can use a technique called box breathing to relieve stress and deal with difficult situations. This technique is also called four-square breathing. To do this, ensure that you are sitting upright in a comfortable chair with your feet flat on the floor in a quiet environment. Place your hands on your lap with the palms facing up and keep your spine straight. First, exhale slowly through your mouth until all the air has left your lungs. Next, inhale slowly and deeply through your nose. Count to four as you feel the air fill your lungs. Hold this breath for a count of four then exhale through your mouth again. Count to four again before you inhale. Repeat this process. This technique's effectiveness lies in being conscious of the feeling of the air moving in and out of your lungs. It promotes the balance of oxygen intake and carbon dioxide expulsion.

Another technique for conscious breathing to handle difficult situations is called the alternate nostril breathing technique. It is a yogic breath control practice and is known as nadi shodhana pranayama in Sanskrit. Directly translated, it means "subtle energy clearing breathing technique." Even though it is typically done as part of a yoga and meditation practice, this conscious breathing technique can be done on its own to help calm your mind.

To practice the alternate nostril breathing technique:

1. Sit in a quiet room with your legs crossed.

2. Place your left hand on your left knee and use the thumb on your right hand to block your right nostril.

3. Inhale through your left nostril then block the left nostril with your fingers.

4. Unblock the right nostril and exhale through this side.

5. Inhale through the right nostril then use your fingers to block them.

6. Open the left nostril and exhale through the left side.

7. Repeat this process for 5 minutes and end the practice by exhaling on the left side.

In addition to helping alleviate stress, the alternate nostril breathing technique helps improve lung function, increase respiratory endurance, and improve cardiovascular function.

Finally, let's discuss the 4-7-8 breathing technique. Based on an ancient yogic technique called pranayama, it is excellent for helping people fall asleep in a shorter time. Adequate amounts of sleep help to fight stress and anxiety. As with the other breathing techniques, to begin the 4-7-8 breathing technique, you need to find a quiet, comfortable place to sit or lie down. If you are using this technique to aid in falling asleep faster, lying down is best. The first thing you need to do is rest the tip of your tongue against your mouth's roof right behind your top front teeth. Keep your tongue in this position throughout the breathing technique.

While it takes some practice to keep your tongue in place while you exhale, you will get it with time. Next:

1. Exhale through your mouth and make a whooshing sound as you let your lips fall apart.

2. Close your lips and inhale silently through your nostrils for a count of four. Hold your breath for 7 seconds.

3. Repeat Step 1. Exhale for 8 seconds.

4. Repeat the entire process for a pattern of 4 breaths.

No matter which technique you use, as you learn how to use your breath to keep calm and relaxed in difficult situations, you will find that you automatically become conscious of your breathing and avoid the negative effects that stress has on it. To compound the effects of conscious breathing, you can use practices such as meditation and mind/body exercises such as yoga and Tai Chi to promote mindfulness and a deeper awareness of the effect that breathing has on your overall being.

Breathlessness

SUMMARY OF BREATH BY JAMES NESTOR. Breathlessness or shortness of breath is a sensation that usually appears in surprising and emotional situations. It happens during the activation of automatic sympathetic nervous system. Sometimes, a person experiences such difficulty when breathing that he/she actually become hungry for air, which is called dyspnea. More often than not, this is due to anxiety behavior. There are three types of irregular breathing due to functional and non-organic conditions. These are psychogenic hyperventilation, psychogenic dyspnea, and compulsive sighing. They all can be referred to as behavioral breathlessness.

Psychogenic hyperventilation is usually linked with momentary events and is not chronic. When a sudden, unexpected, and overwhelming event occurs, a person begins to breathe in shallow breaths, which releases carbon dioxide (CO_2) from the body. The carbon dioxide is crucial in the stimulation of the brain respiratory center to induce and maintain breathing. If a person breathes irregularly, there is a chance for him/her to faint. A person often breathes with their chest instead of with the abdomen (which is healthier). Irregular breathing may appear with other symptoms as well: palpitations, pain in the chest, etc. These episodes of irregular breathing may repeat and force a person to seek a professional opinion on it. It is important to rule out panic attacks and anxiety, and a healthcare provider will ask about specific worrying thoughts and fears. Breathlessness may be associated with twitching of fingers and tingling. This may be due to subconscious stimulation of respiratory center, which then induces a person to over-breathe, and the current situation in the body pushes calcium from the blood into the cells, which causes the twitching and tingling in the extremities.

Compulsive sighing is when a person compulsively breathes more than ordinary person does, and this is due to worrying thoughts of not breathing enough. The need to breathe more appears during emotionally overwhelming situations, when a person tends to make herself better by breathing when actually the opposite happens. It is usual that these episodes last for a couple of weeks, especially while the person is very worried. The cause is hidden in the subconscious and unresolved inner issues and don`t have an explainable organic background.

Breathing disorders that are functional rather than organic, appear much more often in children and adolescents and are linked with some major events (positive or negative). Once they figure out what's triggering it and make a conscious effort to stop it, the symptoms will decrease in adults and young people. These abnormalities in breathing are happening without any organic cause, and are therefore unexplainable, but this behavior can be changed. They are sometimes associated with depression or anxiety, and it was proven that breathing exercises improve breathing and comorbidities.

Trivia Questions

1. Who wrote "Breathe: The New Science of a Lost Art"?

2. What is the name of the device used to stretch the mouth?

3. How did the jaw size of humans change?

4. What is the perfect breath?

5. Do you find it hard to breathe?

6. Which breathing technique are you most interested in trying?

7. Do you believe breathing is the third pillar of health?

Conclusion

SUMMARY OF BREATH BY JAMES NESTOR. "Breath: The New Science of A Lost Art," by James Nestor, was published in May of 2020 by Riverhead Books. It was the #1 Amazon Bestseller in Extreme Sports and Anatomy. It took Nestor over ten years to compile the research needed to publish the book. He currently lives in San Francisco.

James Nestor is an American author and has written for publications such as The New York Times, The Atlantic, Dwell, Scientific American, and Outside. In 2014, he wrote Deep: Freediving, Renegade Science, and What The Ocean Tells Us About Ourselves, which was nominated for a 2015 PEN/ESPN Award for Literary Sports Writing. It also won Amazon's Best Science Book of 2014.

Thank You!

Hope you've enjoyed your reading experience.

We here at Genius Reads will always strive to deliver to you the highest quality guides.

So I'd like to thank you for supporting us and reading until the very end.

Before you go, would you mind leaving us a review on Amazon?

It will mean a lot to us and help us create high-quality guides for you in the future.

Warmly yours,

The **Genius Reads** Team

Made in the USA
Coppell, TX
14 September 2020